Where the Wind Comes From

Where the Wind Comes From

Poems by

Richard Jackson

Cover design by Shay Culligan
Cover art by Terri Harvey, *The Descent* (Acrylic)

ISBN: 978-1-952326-90-5

Kelsay Books
502 South 1040 East, A-119
American Fork, Utah, 84003

Other Books by Richard Jackson

Poems
Take Five (with 4 other poets)
Resonancia (Barcelona)
Out of Place
Traversings (with Robert Vivian)
Retrievals
Resonance
Half Lives
Unauthorized Autobiography
Alive All Day
Falling Stars (Limited Edition)
Svetovi Narazen (Slovenia)
Heart's Bridge (Limited Edition)
Worlds Apart
Part of the Story

Translations
Last Poems: Selected Poerms of Giovanni Pascoli (Italian, with
SusanThomas, Deborah Brown)
Potovanje Sonca (Journey of the Sun) by Alexsander Peršola (Slovene)

Chapbooks
Strays
Fifties
Cesare Pavese: The Woman in the Land (translation)
Greatest Hits 1980–2004

Critical Books and Editions
Dismantling Time in Contemporary American Poetry
Acts of Mind: Interviews with American Poets
The Fire Under the Moon
The Heart's Many Doors
Double Vision: Slovene Poetry
Iztok Osojnik: Selected Poems

There is some link that binds together the making of a poem, the illusions of recall, and the tenuous expectation that somehow we all will hear again the voice that preceded the instauration of a cosmos forlorn and vagrant, through which we blankly wander, unable to distinguish what was said and what we strive to find again.
—Harold Bloom, *Possessed By Memory*

These are the things which you should do: speak the truth to one another; judge with truth and judgement for peace in your gates.

—Zechariah, 8:16 (NASB)

The Other, therefore, is known on account of our responsibility and response to the Other and our judgement by the Other, through which we become responsible to the Other.

—Slavoj Zizek, *The Fragile Absolute*

Acknowledgments

Thanks to the following publications that have graciously granted permission to reprint some of these poems, usually in earlier versions:

Broken Horizons: "The Secret Word-Lot's Wife," "Joseph's Dream," "Balaam's Prophecy," "Ruth's Hope," "Ruth's Advice," "David's Lost Psalm," "Nicodemus' Dream," "Paul's Lesson," "John: The Work of Revelation"

Out of Place: "Jonah's Anger," "Cain's Legacy," "Daniel's Prophecy," "Thomas' Blindness," "Tidings"

Resonance: "Apology of Judas," "The Lesson of Samson"

Heartwall: "Job's Epilogue," "Jeremiah's Lament"

Unauthorized Autobiography: "Cain's Legacy, "

North American Review: "Hosea's Appeal"

Cutthroat: "Naboth's Truth"

Contents

Notes

I began this project accidentally when I was looking for a voice to speak about some of the horrors and injustices in the Balkan wars of the nineties where I was helping in various humanitarian capacities and in writing and creating awareness. "Jeremiah's Lament," was the result. The idea was to have him speak as if he were alive today—with freedom to talk about himself, our world, even the text he finds himself in. But that only started to open up the poems that followed to the nearly infinite issues that surround us: immigration, environment, war, racism and so much more. Why biblical characters? It gave an excuse, I suppose, to speak in moral terms without sounding morally superior myself. In fact, many of the characters admit to their own faults which, I hope, gives them a more authentic and believable voice. They appear here in the order they appear in the literature.

Notes

Prologue: Litany from Before the Beginning

The work is the origin of the artist.
—Heidegger, "The Origin of the Work of Art"

From the dark flower of the black hole desiring to embrace us.
From our galaxy that shudders to shed us after each war.
From the invisible planet we know by its gravity.
From our brittle lives that break apart on moonlight.
From the sirens that slice through the scarves of night.
From the girl shot through her bedroom wall in a drive-by.
From a blink tangled in the eels of the nervous system,
the creeping whispers of the Morning Glory, the solace
of the passerby who places a blanket under the victim's
head, from a man on the streetcar hawking day old
newspapers, and the hawk itself riding sleeves
of wind, from the cemetery wall that fails to keep
death in and the child's first breath that lets death
escape. Everything containing its opposite.
From the unspoken or repressed words of the prophets.
From the mothers uncovering the mass graves
in Srebeniča, Argentina, Berundi, Salvador.
From the lover whose skin ripples at a touch
and whose enormous heart could rival the Killer
Whale's which weighs over a ton. From the smell of
fresh rain on the blacktop roads to galaxies collapsing
into grains of light. Everything exploding into the shape
of hymns. From our lives like jet trails or a father
blowing smoke rings in the shape of a mother's rosary.
From the soldier surprised at how easily the bullet tore
through his flak jacket as he disappeared into
jungle shadows. From the homeless woman
on the subway, her life brimming over her tattered
shopping bags. For Time sweating through the walls
and pipes of our hopes. From the protesters marching
in the streets and across bridges. From the beheadings
that blaspheme the name of God, but also the man

reciting the poem at the poet's grave for he knows
the nightshade has its own time for flowering.
From orchards and tenements, from cloudbursts
and droughts, from lichen, highways, waterfalls,
from the dogwood trying always to straighten itself,
from the new species of ourselves unearthed in Africa,
from Love itself, her knees pulled up, her face glowing
in firelight, her favorite sickle moon cutting a new trail
across the sky, and from our words like heart, like soul,
like prayer, from wonder, from forgiveness,
from everything that knows our love before we do.

Cain's Legacy

You can't stop the boxcars of despair.
You can't stop my voice from hiding out
like a virus inside your words, their knives
clamped between your teeth. You can't stop
the dogs gnawing on the bones from mass graves.
Thus your mirrors holding other faces. Thus your lungs
filled with someone else's words.
The eyelids of the heart closing. The sky drunk
on vapor trails. Otherwise, a few packages of conscience
to the refugees. You can't stop the sounds
of exploding stars as they approach you.
The anxious triggers. The land mines of idealism.
You can't stop Dismay from stumbling
out of the trenches of your dreams.
You can't stop these ghosts sitting around your table
gnawing on the past. Their candles burn down
to shimmering wounds in their cups.
Everyone holding their favorite flags like napkins.
The sound of bugles spilling from the room like laughter.
I know, you kill what you love just to hate yourself
all the more. You put on the cloak of distance.
A wind that blows away the weeks. The lovers' wilted embrace
that was your only, your last hope.
Everyone his own Judas. After a while
even the moon is just an excuse not to look too closely.
You can't stop the past boiling up in the heart like lava.
Otherwise, a history written by shadows.
For example, someone says the universe is expanding,
more anxious optimism, but where would it expand into?
There's only the vacuum that's always inside us.
There's Stephen Hawking saying the past is pear shaped
but that doesn't feed anyone. You can't stop the brain
of the starving child turning into a peach pit,
not his body terrorizing itself for food,

not his face wrinkling like the orange you leave on your table,
his liver collapsing, the last few muscles snug
over his bones like the tight leather gloves of your debutante.
Otherwise your old lies yawning to wake in the corner.
You can't stop the pieces of the suicide bomber
from splattering all over the cafe walls.
You can't stop the walls the tanks crush from rising again.
Otherwise a few tired rivers, a few fugitive stars.
The seasons that ignore us. The cicadas giving up on us.
Hope's broken antennas. Love trying to slip out of the noose.
The betrayed lives we were meant to live.
You can't stop that town from turning its soul on a spit,
not the light chiseling away desire, the morning
wandering dazed through the underbrush of deception.
You can't stop these sails of tomorrow hanging limp
from their masts. All you have are these backwaters of touch,
this voice spinning like a broken compass,
this muzzle made from your own laws.
But you can't stop the bodies piling up.
You can't stop the deafening roar of the sky.
You can't stop the bullet you've aimed at your own head.

Jonah's Anger

You look at the sky and see clouds, I see
the footsteps of sinners. I see Justice shivering
in some of your abandoned buildings.
All night the darkness looks for the pain
it belongs to. And me? I told a whole city
it was doomed. How could He forgive
their sins filling the air like shrapnel? Retribution
leaked through the sieve holes of the stars.
Nineveh. My words were drowned by mercy,
and weeds entangled my dreams. Why
should sinners live, why weren't their bones
scattered like dice? Their souls were empty
bottles trying to sing in the wind. Your own
souls kill themselves for the sound of a phrase
or a god. Each promise you make is a landmine.
Each hope labeled with a date of expiration.
How few of you have ever understood
that the scents you set your dogs on are your own?
Your own scientists tell you that your visions are
the result of damaged brains, no more real
than phantom limbs. Even Kierkegaard called
what he dreaded *dream*. He watched his father
curse God from a hilltop which made him famous.
Forget how his family then died from God's wrath,
forget how he abandoned his love for his books.
Like you, he thought prophecy was nothing special.
You see a bird or a country caught in a thornbush
and you think you know what happens next.
Why should you listen? Someone tells you
that the recent deformities in frogs are clues
for what happens next to you, as scripture says,
and you laugh. But I tell you, only what forgets you is real.
All you think about is my whale, the fish.
All I knew was the immense loneliness wherever

my shadow tried to escape me. I wanted to be
thrown overboard. Later to be burnt in a desert.
There was His lesson I still don't understand.
There was His presence, a doorway that always stood
beside me. I swear each turn of the knob is blasphemy.
Now I am one of you. In the end,
it is not the world that is so distasteful,
but life itself. Even today,
whole countries slowly fade like bruises,
and we never learn. In the end, the frost collects
around our eyes. And heaven? Our heaven is
the boarded up tenement you pass without pausing.

Abraham's Journey

Sorrow walked in my clothes before I did. Flocks
of shadows followed me. One night I looked at the stars
I thought were gods until they disappeared. Some say
I smashed my father's idols and walked away.
Or walked towards a desert of barren promises.
Or promises that are hummingbirds hovering for
a moment then drifting away. Even now, walking
towards that mountain, sometimes I will watch
my shadow sitting beneath a plane tree, casting dice,
ignoring my steps. Some of you made me a founder
but it was only that shadow. Some of you made me
your father, but it was yourselves you were describing.
You plant a tree, you dig a well, and it brings life,
that's all. Everything else is the heart's mirage.
Except what begins inside you. Except Sarah.
When she stepped inside my dream the curtains
shivered, whole mountains entered the room.
It always seemed a question of which love to honor.
The land I loved fills with fire. Who should we listen to?
It's true, He offered the world and I offered only
myself. But I thought His words were coffins. I was
frantic for any scrap of shade. Now everything is
shade. Your old newspapers are taken up by the wind
like pairs of broken wings. Each window, each door is
a wound. One track erases another track. One bomb.
One rock, one rubber bullet. What can I tell you?
Where have you left your own morning of promises?
You remember Isaac, maybe Ishmael, but not the love
that led me there. Not Sarah. Just to hear the sound
of her eyelids opening, or her plants pushing the air
aside as they reach for the sun, twilight filling
her fingers like fruit. This afternoon a flock of doves

settled on my porch. Their silence took the shape
of all I ever wanted to say. Today, the miracle
you want aches inside the trees. Why believe
anything except what is not believable? I never
thought of it as a trial, not any of it. Now the leaves
turn into messages that are only impossible to read.
The roots turn into roads as they break through
the surface. How can I even know what I mean?
Beneath the hem of night the rain falls asleep
on the grass. We have to turn into each other.
One heart inside the other's heart. One love. One word.
Inside us, our shadows will walk into water,
the water will walk into the sky. Blind. Faithful.
Inside us the music turns into a flock of birds.
Theirs is a song whose promise we must believe
the way the moon believes the earth, the fire believes
the wood, that is, for no reason, for no reason at all.

Isaac's Consent

Why did the silence lay heavy on his shoulder?
Why did the animals we passed close their eyes in shame?
For a while the land had no horizon. For that while
he never trusted me, never thought I might consent.
We never see the storms loitering behind the mountains
with almost too much to say. For three days
I carried the bowl of fire. Time seemed to rise
like its smoke. I watched the locusts
clinging to blades of grass. On the first day,
there was a small boy, puzzled, who thought
he could put the morning moon in a bucket.
On the second day, a beggar slipped off his stool
because he knew the answers to everything
I asked. On the third, I knelt on the wood pile.
The ram caught in the bushes was no concern of mine.
We only see what we want to see, hear what we want to hear.
The prisoners you mistreat are no concern of yours.
Everyone is a victim. No difference. Even today, your soldiers
talk to a blind Tomorrow that disappears down some
sniper alley, or turns its back on them, or plants
a roadside mine. Even your flags can't be trusted.
I wanted only that there be no more silences.
I wanted my father, and you, to say what you mean.
To find a word for our faith older than faith.
Does the future always have to flash like a knife?
Do we always have to create dreams from our histories?
What escapes you, never leaves you. Everything is
a journey of trust. You have to have the kind of faith
the flame has for the candle, that the bird has for its wings.
Otherwise, our words have no destinations.
Otherwise, our words are snakes that swallow our souls.
Today, I heard the river empty itself of its memories.
I knew I would have to tell you all of this.
I think I could speak with the voice of the ram.

The Secret Word: Lot's Wife

How could anyone not look back? Not even darkness
Could have closed my eyes. I became the salt
of the earth, as your saying goes. But Lot never even
noticed me the next day. Salt of the earth. How could
anyone? The sun rose as usual. Cities shimmered
in the distance. I stood there like Eurydice as the earth
exploded. The sand is there only to explain the wind.
The hills ignore the valleys. The moon disowns its own
origins. The only life we have is history. But you are
afraid to look at your own past, your massacres for
your god or country, the hungry you ignore, the land
you kill. Salt of the earth. Next year's moths are waiting
in cocoons you nurtured yesterday. Who is anyone without
a desire to see what happens? You fill your clocks with
pictures that are out of focus. Everything you do provokes
the stars. That is why their cryptic alignments refuse
to give warnings. And the one word you have tried all
your lives to say dies on our lips as you die. It blows away
with the desert sand. Why do you believe your own words?
When was it your own Jesus called his disciples
the salt of the earth? My own names are on parole.
You turn your histories into anecdotes or slogans.
The horizon has crumbled. The weight of the sky is
nearly unbearable. All your signposts are blank.
The rags of forgotten flags litter your fathers' lands.
Your truth is what you believe, but it is only a distorted
carnival mirror. That's why there is always that unwanted
stranger, who looks away, lurking behind the subjects of
your photos. He steals the scene the way I steal your thoughts.
You say peace but mean war, love but mean power.
In the end you will forget your own names. Some
scribes have called me Edith. You can look it up.

It is just a word, and of no consequence. History says
I should warn you, and have. There. As if it would do
any good. Like me you'll turn and look. Like I did
you'll see only what you want to see, name only
what you want to name. Salt of the earth.

Jacob's Fear

I have lived too long as a prisoner of clouds.
They float like clothes strung over the barbed wire
from one of your camps, a story that has no words.
I don't even know if these dreams are my own.
What I know is based on what is not there: a shadow
behind a wavering curtain in a fifth floor walk-up,
a mirror filled with disbelief, the dark spaces
between stars. What is it that any of us fights with
except what betrays us, and what betrays us is
what we are. My own sons knew nothing but revenge
for their sister and wiped out a town. There is a shame
that is the hidden face of the world. It is all betrayal.
All we can do is limp through history. Every bone is
a kind of crutch. After a while I became only a few words
scribbled to mean whatever you want them to mean.
Sometimes I believe the only truths worth reading are
spray painted on overpasses and the rocky sides of hills.
Other times I remember the face I fought and what it said.
It's been a longtime passing and I am still not sure
what it all meant. There was a blessing. There was
a change. And still there is the empty cave inside of me.
The afternoon walks through fields like a farmer whose
crops have failed. This is not what you wanted to hear,
and frankly, you need a kind of stage manager to keep
all this straight. I too once thought our dreams escaped
to inhabit other souls when we died. I too thought that
the bodies at Babi Yar, arranged so efficiently so as not
to have to dig too deep, was a moment, a displaced
fragment of history. One time I knew exactly what to do.
One time I thought it was just God's punishment
the way your preacher's justify bombings and tornadoes,
or the gassing of whole Syrian or Kurdish villages,

as something deserved. How perverse to excuse
one nightmare with another. Who would want that God?
Now I am just tired of revenge. Why should our words be
indictments, our lives summarized on Police blotters.
Time is tired of being time. What does the fish think
as it leaves the water, and the insect at that very moment?
Does it matter that this is the only mystery worth knowing?
Each millennium the planets create a new geometry of the sky.
The question is, will any of this change us. Will it stop
the stars from turning their backs on us? Once, back then,
they changed my name, but I left a shadow there. Now
I am afraid our dreams wait, quivering, hanging from skies
like those bats infected with fungus in caves we can't explore.

Joseph's Dream

That deep in the pit I could see the hidden dreams
of daylight stars. If I listened carefully, I could hear
the earth's plates grumbling. I didn't know why.
Every once in a while a grudging wind might twist
its way down to me. Every once in a while a raindrop
would leave its thumbprint in the mud. I learned, then,
that our real histories lie in wait in the shadows.
My own brothers tried to kill or sell me, you know
the story. Revenge crumbled from the dirt walls.
But it's true, I was unfair. I thought to imprison
them. I dreamt the sheaves and stars bowed
down to me. My own words became my chains.
I was ashamed. What I can't decipher is your own
cavernous dreams. They have no meanings that don't
spread out like the tracks of a frightened herd towards
wars, rapes, beheadings and the refugees from the everyday
selling of lives. You thought you could put the moon
in a prison. You called arrogance by the name of
practicality. The books you held sacred you refused
to follow. Pretty soon another day is out of reach.
The whole planet's reflected light is so dim it too
is invisible from the stars. The whole universe
surrounds us like a ring of toadstools that hide
their secret connections beneath the earth.
What will you dream when your words are forgotten?
This morning I watched as a stray dog settled into sleep
among the worn headstones. I do not know whether
he was remembering or forgetting. I think we have to
burrow deep into our own dreams, into the pits of
our worst desires. We have to gather every syllable

in search of a truer meaning. Sometimes our dreams
seek sanctuary in what we can't say. Why can't we
clothe our hearts in each others' hearts? My dream
eddies out of the coves and inlets of these words. Here,
a firefly copies, now and then, the ashes of a dying star.

Moses' Revision

You shall remember that you were an alien
In the land of Egypt, therefore I am
Commanding you to do this thing.
                              —Deut 24:21-22

I was always an illegal alien. I never knew God.
For some I was an Egyptian, for others an outsider,
for others a Hebrew. Who ever knows who they are?
Our stories are the myths that seem to write themselves:
I won a war by holding up my arms, or split the seas.
In truth, I was a victim of my own stories. I killed a man,
a guard, because I thought of the man he was beating
as a brother. In the desert there are voices everywhere.
The sound of light as it bakes the earth, stars scuffing
the sky, water whispering not far beneath our feet.
Yesterday's clouds leave their thumbprints on the sky.
Everything is a metaphor. Our lives are metaphors.
The sun rises on a pillar of light. The birds arrive before
dawn with their secret messages. Everything is a mystery:
water from rocks, bushes that speak through their flames.
What can you do but believe? For all I did, I doubted
only once. Another time He tried to kill me for forgetting
who I am, just one soul among the souls of the earth.
His ways are his ways. It's like trying to explain why
he lets the moon blot out the sun. In the end, I wrote
what I saw but never understood. I was wrong.
What I took for an enemy was a mirage. It was we
who invaded. It was we who came in on the migrant wind.
Now you think you know what I meant, but your own words
cast endless shadows. Everyone has their Golden Calves.
You hoard yours behind the darker walls of your hearts.
You would have cast me back across your borders.
We were all migrants then, we are all migrants now.

I have my visions and now my revisions. We were chosen not
to destroy but to reveal, to warn. A handful among the grains
of the earth, a galaxy among the stars. In the end I cursed
some of you, but that, too, was wrong. We curse ourselves,
yet I see now, beyond the land I could not enter, the far lands
you have made: shadows without bodies, black holes for souls.

Balaam's Prophecy

Yes, we were always handcuffed to our old habits.
Yes, to see the truth is to look through tracing paper.
In the end, my life was worth the same as roadkill.
Because of me the sky seems pockmarked with stars.
Ravens turn the trees black. Our sins are laid out like
fish at the market. There were signs, yes, but me, I
prophesized a whole nation against itself and thousands
fell by the plague. I had hoped no one would remember.
It wasn't only what I believed, but what I didn't believe.
It wasn't only what I did, but what I didn't do. I should have
helped the Moabites to change. I should have heard
an Angel and not a donkey. What you don't want
to see is not a reason to close your eyes. Listen
to the leaves that curl into themselves, then fall. And you,
your own bullets turn the air to lace and then you want
to sell the lace. You peel away the souls of the poor.
You dress the rich in fine excuses. You aren't any
different. Your past plays in the background like
a drummer's soft brushing. Your history is
a criminal who has escaped. I have no faith in your words
that drift about like smoke. What I was told to tell you
I told to Barak—that the world you are about to make is
not the world you think, that the vaults of your ears are closed,
the doors of your eyes locked shut, that the corridors of
your hearts are hordes for your profits, that your souls are
laced with blind excuses. In the end, you have to choose.
A vulture sweeps its black hand over the far field.
A dove alights on the garden wall as if remembering the flood.

Rahab's Resistance

Joshua 2

My own guilt was long wedged in my heart.
Not for my city whose smoke rose into incoherence.
Not for the men who brought a truth that was real.
Our life for yours was what they asked, but
it wasn't just my life, nor my family's, it was
the belief they came from God. I knew then
the soot had been lifted from my heart. I let
them down with a scarlet rope when the guards left
though I knew then how some would call me a traitor.
I could see the black branches of a tree web the air.
Paraphrases of moonlight fell on the city walls.
Later, leaving the rope as a sign, there was a sound
that turned stone into sand that I don't understand.
I am not a traitor. Sometimes a whole city
can be wrong, a whole country and its king.
You can resist or you can wait as the whole sky
breaks apart above you. Don't wait. It takes
no prophet to see where you are headed,
your leaders hiding behind sandstorms of deceptions.
They will divide you so that in the end you will deny
yourself. In the end it would be your own death
that is chiseled on your soul. Don't wait.

Nathan: Speaking Truth to Power

In truth, his great heart was a weathervane.
He followed the faded tracks of illusory animals,

mistook frost crystals for stars, reflections over
the things themselves. No leader is a leader

who sends a man alone to the front lines in order
to claim his widow. You have to say something.

I told him the story of the rich man claiming
the flock of the poor, but what I meant was him.

Who did that, he asked. *You are the man,* I said.
Then the wind shaped a hand slapping his face.

And you, what truths have you said or done?
Your own kings have stories like clouds of locusts.

Their words create endless box canyons.
Their words are mudslide covering whole villages.

You have to speak from where the wind comes from,
to risk your words falling like stones into the river,

before you appear like a mirage on the desert floor,
before your own words become homeless, your

shadows misshapen, and before you, too,
are deported into a language you no longer speak.

Naboth's Truth

There are always shards of light that are never
swept away. There are so many pages missing
from our histories. Even now the words for Truth
lie muted by the roadside. Newspapers filled with stories
you should read float over you like hawks. Like me,
you don't want to believe. They say I cursed God
to stone me and steal my garden. My own people!
It was a king who thought you could do anything.
But you know that, and you have one like that
of your own. It was his wife who plotted with two
liars to accuse me. Everyone believed what they wanted
to believe. Even your own truths seem to dart
in and out of sight like fireflies. The lies hover
like yellow jackets around the garbage. What
you will be left with is something like the shells
left after the pigeons in the park. Our prophet
sounded like an owl in the night, but the king
would not listen until the truth finally ended him.
It was dogs that licked the blood of his wife.
But that is not my truth. I live in a waking landscape.
My soul hovers over you still, like a dragonfly.
It wasn't just a garden it was a history, the story
of my family. We do not have long. In a while
you will hear the sound of locusts stirring beneath
your feet, but you may not know it. There is no truth
that will not upset you. It doesn't care what you think.
Like the rogue planets spun off from dying stars,
invisible now, until they will, like the Truth, collide
with everything you thought you once believed.

Jael's Defense

...let me trust my heart that not in vain
I've reached out with my words to touch [the world]
      —Amir Or, Prayer 4

Yes, but who knows where the wind comes from.
Likewise, who knows what voice told me to act.
Yes, I took the hammer and drove the tent peg
through his skull. You have your own stones
and tanks and missiles. He was warned by Deborah.
The bones on the battlefield had turned into roots.
His iron chariot had already turned to rust in the wadi.
Yes, I broke hospitality. And yes, my husband's
treaty. Yes, it was not my place as a wife, but, yes,
it was. Who tells the stars what constellation to join?
His dreams forgot their meanings and lay down
in the coffins they made. There is the law in the scrolls
and the law in my heart. You know, you have your own
tyrants. Yes, he wanted asylum and water and I gave him
a skin of milk before the wind came and plundered
my heart. What it took was not justice but collusion.
You understand. What you do not have lies everywhere
at your feet. There are these houses crumbling from lies.
There are these words crumbling like rocks on the sea cliffs.
There are, despite all this, lives still crumbling from blame
and hate. And yes, there are voices we hear that put an end
to death through Death itself. If you knew the word I use for *yes*,
you could hear in it the pulse of my own heart. His words
were frozen in the wrong time. My *yes* lives beyond words.
By morning the clouds rose over the mountains like
the Hand of God. Yes, it may be I inherit the stain,—no,
a shadow, but also the light that creates the shadow,
the shadow of the cloud I cannot, no, can never name.

Micah's Prophecy

Time subsides and you fall back into the hammock
of another easy truth. There are so many ways to
disguise this. One reigning idea dictates what you will
think, and so you go blundering from one war to another,
one rape or abuse to another. My dream for you is clothed
with shadows. Listen,—your final dawn will arrive rudely.
What became of me wasn't worth the telling. But, I'll say
this: the real dungeons are our own words, the real chains
are the ones we use to encircle our own hearts. There are
letters in my alphabet you'll never know. I saw a whole
army collapse like a huge lung. I saw bodies fall like
chips from a woodsman's axe. There was a king who
believed me, and one who didn't. You know their fates.
Your own kings pencil in their beliefs for later erasure.
After each tragedy they hand out antique apologies.
Thoughts and prayers, you say, echoing an empty cavern.
Your mouths have the shapes of the end of a muzzle.
Your eyes are gunsights, your ears are petrified wood.
Someone shoots in a theater and soon it plays like fiction.
Someone else pulverizes symbols they don't understand.
When you break the world it doesn't just get fixed.
You have no idea how many things you've become
a symbol for. Your answers explode like terrorist bombs.
There is a truth, if you listen, but it arrives with no
postmark and no return address, no provision for revision.
Even your windows mutter things you refuse to understand.
I can say: there is little patience with your skeletal words.
I can say: you should already know this by reading
what has already been written on the dungeon walls of
your own hearts and the watermarks of your own souls.
The harp plays on, but the question is, who's listening?

Elijah's Warning

Why does the soul, like a startled dove, flee from itself?
Why do we live so often in the dark caves of the heart?
These are the questions that nest like a tangle of spiders.
A man rises from the subway vent to a world that has
abandoned the world—to draw his lost life over a billboard
picture of a life he'll never know. Listen, there are storms
that shred mountains. There are rocks that shake themselves
as the earth splits. There are my words that you burned
to ashes now floating aimlessly. No one wanted to listen.
How easy it is to hope the clouds wash away the sky's light.
We have become so inventive in our cruelties—as today
a flash of shrapnel flies through a hospital ward, someone
drives a car into a crowd, an ISIS sniper welcomes the challenge
of a child's small head, another child is hollowed out by
a gang bullet from beyond her bedroom wall. No one wants
to listen. Ages ago I told the king what would happen.
Now, I'm telling you: your own kings are leading you
to dreams that are not dreams with words that are not words,
hopes that are not hopes. No one seems to understand
the shimmer of light that surrounds you before the lightning
strikes. Your excuses rise from the trees like vultures. No one
understands the script for their own roles drawn on abandoned
walls. But there's no language, no image that won't tell you what
I mean. Listen to the pain of the hills as they are torn apart
for a few dollars and whose veins are piped with poisons. Listen
to the cry of the child caught in the rubble of a suburban meth lab.
Listen: you have to hear more than you can hear. You can't really
understand until you hear the weight of pollen as it falls to earth,
the sound the moon makes dragging its pale, almost invisible
light, across the daytime sky, the way you push the air apart as you
walk, which is the soul's breath leaving or entering, which is
your breath as it sifts through the caves of your lungs. Listen.

Ruth's Hope

*Judge not, that you be not judged. For with what judgment
you judge, you will be judged; and with the measure you
use, it will be measured back to you.*
                                        —Matthew 7:1, NKJV

Today it would be Jordan. I would wear a head scarf.
It would be the same sun eating the dirt, making thorns
of the air. I left my people yes, but love them still, while
their lands are bulldozed, the same lands you once
exiled them to, where my husband lay. Because you left
the fallen grain for the poor I went to gather it. It is
that same dust that seasons our food, the same wind
that is sandpaper on the face. You could map my journey
by its tendrils of pain. I was still a foreigner. I was
ready to pull down the clouds around me. But I knew
that the new belief was tolerance. What has happened?
The birds and snakes have become planes and tanks.
The words you once used to embrace have changed into
words that will strangle you. My own words were not
ones you'd listen to—a woman's, but still, they hovered
over you like a mindful moon behind a haze of clouds.
My own road took me to a Bethlehem before yours.
My own road took me to a husband whose words
shaded mine as mine shaded his despite your laws.
Everyone is a migrant. Even the stars turn in circles.
This morning a sparrow pecking uselessly
for worms would not give up, its wings fluttering like
a heart. It paid no attention to the contrails of jets.
The face of the desert has a look this evening that
I would like to call home, that I would like to call love.

Ruth's Advice

Did it matter if my blood was streaked like one of
those streams that stumble by our broken world?
I stepped into the field like a field until he nearly
tripped over me. You know nothing of real solitude—
your stories and your mirrors keep you company.
Why can't you go wherever your love goes, live
wherever your love lives? If you are going to love
you have to be ready to sacrifice everything. I could have
returned to comfort in Jerusalem, not lived among
those people I hardly knew. I loved all that I loved.
I worked everything that needed to be worked:
It wasn't my grain but what that grain could mean.
In the end all our lives are strewn across the road
like curls of one of your truck's blown tires.
What's to salvage? Look around us all now.
Sometimes we don't even know what you thirst for.
We think we can give yourself over to the wind.
Don't you think the bed sheets scorched my skin?
I lay at Boaz' feet and, startled, he covered me. I put
my mouth to his heart. The night tilted away from us.
I became one of you. You became one of me. But
I never understood how you could hang someone's words
like a man from a tree, or just even refuse someone
a place to sit. In the long run it leads to the way we can
refuse the women in Darfur raped by the Junjaweed,
Devils on Horseback. And the children, thousands,
chased by government planes that slash the skin of the sky,
armored jeeps in a country that is a storm of vultures,
a chain of coffins. Each time we turn away we bruise
our own souls. Each time we turn away our own death
drifts like fallout through our hearts. What do we want?
Where are we if we can't love the worst of us?

What are we if we can't try to mend the dusk's bleeding sky?
What are we if we can't love more than the world allows,
more than the odor of fig trees that fills the night air,
more than the late swallows that circle, embracing the last tree?

The Lesson of Samson

What do you do when your shadow is more exact than
your own self? When your own secrets sleep in your throat?
Even the nightingale sings what it collects from the day's
failures. There was a time when everything pleased me,
When everything called my name. That was before I lived
In a landscape someone else invented. Later, I never found
any certain record of what I was supposed to do,
or why. The key was silence as Manoah tried to tell me
but every word I spoke became an ending. I was just
an echo with no first sound. I was alone.
Yes, it's true, Deliah was only the last of too many
lovers. (Your own leaders *make no bones,* as you say,
about it.) Inside them, the folds of the universe seemed to
cover me like silk. I went to them because
my own wife betrayed my secret to her friends.
That's why I dragged the burning fox through their fields.
In the end, we weave our own pain into our lives.
That's why I believe my own shadow felt the wound
when they burned her alive as a kind of revenge,
an act you think savage, but look at your own dirty wars.
We live by symbols and gestures whose meaning
drifts like leaves on the wind. So maybe the lion meant me,
the honey what she could have been. Whatever my life was
supposed to mean crested too far out to sea. Whoever wrote
my story said my own revenge was the hand of God.
Then why the symbol of the jawbone? He said I brought
down the temple of the Infidels, but who is to say
that their souls did not bud like flowers in the fields?
In truth, no revenge, no cause is that noble.
In truth, anyone's knees will bend like stalks of wheat.
Now your own soldiers warm their hands over the bodies
Of children in Angola or my own Palestine.
The hoot of the owl tells us all what we have lost.
And me, I have only these lidless eyelids of desire

to guide me. All I can do now is mimic the roots
that finger, like lovers, the desert sands for water.
Antlers of smoke rise from the cities I razed.
Your own torn cities are burning themselves.
Fear darts in and out of the cellars and ditches.
What did it mean? What could any of us expect?
In the end, you all go back to your idols, the rapes,
the revenge, your bayonets waving like flags,
your words that lie patiently in wait like snipers.
My own face is covered by the sheet of the sky.
Reason leaks from my words. A life is not a life until you die.

Job's Epilogue

The stars prowled my skin but all I wanted
in the end was to see His face. I never doubted
when the rivers that I knew as him dried up.
Why did he want to stay so hidden? Blake says
you can see Him in every grain of sand. There is
a million mile high tornado wandering through
the Lagoon galaxy that might be Him. There are
these icicles reaching desperately for the earth
that may also be Him. Now all I see is an old man
called Death standing under the storefront light
across the street clipping his nails. Does it matter?
All love turns into a beetle in the end. You have
to crush the shell with your heel to survive.
My own friends were a broom to any hope.
They watched me pass through time like a body
caught under the thickening ice until Spring.
They tossed their words like salt on my garden.
They called themselves allies but they were planting
the explosives of revenge like terrorists.
They thought every sickness was a sin.
They thought they could cloak their own guilt
in words that surrounded me like clouds of insects.
They wanted to grab my soul by its throat.
Now they are rolling up your field maps,
looking for a destiny shaped like a conquerable
country, shaped even like the Afghan boy
whose hands have been cut off for stealing
food, like the girl nailed to the door in Bosnia.
Their words siphoned the air around me until
there was only stone. I could see the moon
turn its back to me. I could see the empty trains

leaving the camps, the minefields sprouting
like newly planted crops. They wanted to leave me
lying dead on my own body. My soul was
playing tug of war with the wind. There was never
any meaning to any of it was what the beetles knew.
I'm not saying you don't have any choice but
we get poured out like milk, then thicken like curds.
In the end, all we can drink are our own regrets.
If we were pieces of straw we'd be hunted down.
Their armies are toppling minarets and burning churches.
What good is it to let our thoughts burn like a naked
bulb in the prisoner's room? Eternity has a few more
words to say. I have more than I ever had, but less.
I could see the birds falling from my trees like leaves.
I could see my cup filling with shadows. I could see
the sun was only another kind of cage. What did
He think I would do with all I saw? Hope put away
its watch. Whenever I asked, His ears were full
of darkness. He thought I wanted to harness the stars.
He thought I wanted to teach the grasshopper to leap.
All I wanted in the end was to see his face. You can
hear each new idea rumbling over the horizon. It is written
somewhere that I am each one of you, that the moths
of despair have eaten away our desires, that our hopes
have turned to scar tissue and harden, but it isn't true.
We have to understand the sunlight as a way to cast shadows.
We have to touch each others' shadows like our own.
We have to understand each heart is a kind of cave.
We have to let the bats of hatred fly out of those caves.

David's Lost Psalm

Winter's net of black branches has begun to haul in
a few buds and leaves. There's nothing to explain
our desire to embrace all that surrounds us. A sudden
sun has made the statues glisten. *I was the man,*
as Nathan said, which proved a burden. I remember
my own age of cries as dreadful as yours. We all desired
a story different than the one we lived. I sang
whatever was true, however painful or torturous,
not to dwell in those valleys but to climb out of them.
No one wanted to remember the wars, the captivity,
the rapes. No one wanted to remember that we too
did unspeakable crimes. Now your own stories are
so light they drift away like milkweed looking for
some better ground. There isn't any, there never is.
The moon's scarred face gives us back our souls.
Saul thought I would drift away, then tried to kill me.
I forgave him as I forgave myself. Or wanted to.
Each act leaves a footprint neither the wind nor
the sea can sweep away. My own faults now
crumble like pages of a forgotten passion.
You must think of me as a predator. This is why
I sing, as a much a dream as song. All I know is
that memory is a place that is nowhere, which is why
we can retrieve the lives we never lived. Each song is
a woods where the paths return always to the beginning.
I sing to invent what I can not remember, or to remember
what I can not invent. It is the only way to let my soul
glisten as if it knew. Here a few deer step out of the woods.
The cornstalk stubble has been burnt away. The cemetery
stones are telling only a part of the story but that seems
enough. A sudden wind nudges the statues awake.

Jeremiah's Lament

They said my voice was the storm that gathers in the flower.
They said my words covered the fields like locusts.
Whatever they said, I never wanted to stand apart, even
when they buried me under stones shaped from their hearts.
Yes, midnight clung to my lips, yes inside my mouth the stars
trembled, but who really listened? All they heard was
their own guilt crying inside them like caged birds.
Did what I say come true? Evil lurked in their wells.
God picked them clean the way a shepherd picks his cloak
clean of vermin. In the end, they gasped for air like jackals.
And truth in all this? You yourself have your physics
for the world,—quarks, for example, a matter of
mere logic to some, a real image to others. It only matters
that you believe. You have your own histories
strangling you like vines. For instance, 1597: the year
of the first military field hospitals, the year Spain
and France began peace talks, or the year Samurai warriors
brought back barrels filled with 100,000 noses and ears
from Korea to Kyoto. In Mostar they are still digging under
the rubble of someone's false prophecy. They are looking
for the truth that bursts from a hand grenade. We listen
only to history's megaphone, not the words that splinter
on whispers. We are all turning on a potter's wheel
that shapes one ethnic cleansing after another.
I wanted common words that would laugh and weep at once,—
the fig trees that ripen as the mountains tremble,
the wolves of our desire whose voice flowers in the forest.
But these are the words that put me in jail, words
that lashed my own back, that seared my eyes, words that
still nest in the desert cactus. You call it beautiful, but
the song of the nightingale is only the pain

of never finding its own voice. Still,
everything speaks if you listen closely enough:
the desert dunes sing and moan, shout and stammer
under the weight of their own shifting sands, bees
make a map of air currents by beating their wings.
And my dreams? I dreamt God's judgment
in an almond rod, the city as a boiling pot, and I am
still waiting to see what they mean. I was
promised a bronze-walled city to protect me.
I was promised that the doors of Love would fly open.
Foggy with desire, we have to make our own truths.
All I can tell you is how it is your most precious Hope
that catches on the brambles, that blooms with each rain.
Imagine the stars filling the bottom of your glass.
I swear to you, the sun surrendering itself to darkness
beyond the tree line is the most poignant of moments.

Daniel's Prophecy

Someone is grinding up daylight.
There are a few refugee words slipping across your borders.
It is not the bronchia of the dead tree filling with cicadas.
It is not Nebuchadnezzar. It is not Darius.
The leaves are flecked with rust. Night spreads
its wings with the owl. I was not supposed to tell
you anything until the end. I am only God's skillet.
I am God's butterfly. I hope
you can ransom some hope from the dark.
Sometimes I think my words have harpooned stars.
Sometimes they are just a pin on a general's map.
Everything repeats the shape of death—
the hawk slipping off the edge of the sky,
salmon falling into the rapids,
the hunched snail, our own hunched dreams.
I used to think everything was only a dream—
I once told a king his own dreams as I was
instructed, but I was only repeating a voice
that evaporated like water from the river.
Who was I, who didn't even have my own name?
What did it mean when the clouds
clotted over the mountains? What did it mean
to have a shadow cast all around us?
What does it mean now when Terror writes its name
on the walls from Angola to Afghanistan and no one notices.
Who of us is not guilty of everything?
At least in those days someone would ask.
Now our old words pray over the grave of our ideals.
Isn't it our own young girl in her greasy room
bleeding to death from a coat hanger,
the bloated stomach of our starving infant,
our suicide's razor cutting the wind?

There's no better way I could bundle these words
for you to hear. It is a package you, too, are afraid to open.
It is a mirror in the room of the blind man.
You will not easily escape from its web.
You might as well try to divert
our sniper's bullet from the hill above Tetova, Macedonia.
You might as well try to gather the parts of the boy that are
strewn all over our shelled out-house above that town,
whose bicycle spins its wheels at the moon.
It makes no difference if our pockets are
jammed with good intentions.
We play with history the way the punk works
the pinball machine in the bar down the street.
We have already scattered our hopes like feed for hens.
In all this time, listen, you haven't said a word.
Even the silence of our nails is suspect.
The footprints of our lies cover the ground before us.
It is easy enough to step from the fire
but hard to step out of our words.
I say *we* because here we are
at the end already, and nothing is answered.
It was always the lion's den inside me that I feared.
It was always the lion's den,
and this death not even our God could share.

Hosea's Appeal

Therefore the land mourns, and all who live in it languish;
together with the wild animals and the birds of the air,
even the fish of the sea are perishing.

—Hosea 4:3

If you would listen, you could hear
the White-Browned Sparrow Weavers
sing duets so precise their brains work
as one, like the partners they are. You
can see them resting on the fence rail
that is pushed up like the arthritic back
of an old man, or from a branch that leans
down as if to whisper its own warnings
to the earth. But you have to look, and
you have to listen. This, too, is a vision
beyond sight. Know that they only sing in
your disappearing wild, not in the world
you have rusted like your iron cities.
The lost elms were a warning. The beautiful
red sky that opens its hands to you
in the morning comes not from itself
but the billion particles that poison it.
I can tell you now: you are smelting
your own hearts, your souls. But those
birds, their sounds translate the sounds
of stars at a pitch you can never hear.
Even your physics tells you every atom
sings to every other atom. That's
a parable you haven't really learned.
You could have read it in Humbolt.
You could have read it in Blake—
Everything that Lives is Holy.
When you see the moon scarred
by the broken branches of a tree

take it as a warning. When you see
a star burning out, remember
the retreat of forests into the desert.
When you mistake the horn of a truck
for the song of a bird, it is already over.

Tidings

1. The Annunciation: Her Response

Like a sentence you discover and read after too many
years, after you think the world's heart has turned
to dust, the air shriveling in your lungs, though
you cannot understand some of the words
for they seem like stars with no owners,
something like the ache of flowers for their seeds,
and you begin to realize it is a sentence
that celebrates what you could only imagine
like the canticles of mountain streams,
despite the black hearts perched, years later, on branches,
despite the moon thinning with hunger
then bloating like a starving child,
despite the tracer rounds streaming
like dandelion seeds the Child will blow across His room,
this sentence with its riverbed of stars,
this sentence that carries you too
the way a leaf is pulled downstream, because this,
you begin to realize, is not the song of a seed
fallen on stone, not some light scorched
into the dunes of the sky, but a phrase
whose wings fill the room, and you,—
you are that word which had remained
unnoticed in this sentence, and you begin
to speak with that light that quivers
like a branch, your own lips slightly moving
like a petal the bee has just left,
and you begin to realize you have lived
your whole life in this sentence
gradually unfolding towards its end,
the way the moon now plows the sky,
the way what you once thought was a mere star
now turns out to be a galaxy.

2. Observations of the Three Kings

The sound was all yellow, the flower of the moon
opened. For a while we thought we were living
in the landscape of someone else's dream.
There was a fire that burned like an icicle from a rope.
Someone else said it might be a star.
He seemed to know something about the moon's scars,
so we followed. We tracked the ruts of the sky's song.
You can cut off the branches of a dogwood and still
see its outlines in the air. Sometimes our gaze
just crawled along the road carrying a burden
we somehow wanted. We knew how tight
the chains of our hearts held us.
When we went to the king you could hear the stars wilt.
We thought he wanted to tear the clouds from the sky.
The winds gathered in the mountains, plotting.
We could hear the cry of the trees, the desperate
snail clinging to a rock. Later we heard
the voice of mothers raging over the hills
like the glow of a fire. Everyone we met wanted
to blindfold the sky. It seemed there were clocks
inside their hearts. It seemed their eyes
were made of dust. When we finally arrived
it was as if we could see every blade of grass,
every seed's beginning, every cricket's song,
every star's desire. And then we could speak.
It seemed His words opened our own mouths.
Here was the universe in a husk of song.
Here was a city in a splinter of joy.
Here were our souls embracing like our smoky breaths.
Here was pure hope flowering in His eyes.

3. Joseph's Account

And so the stars finally pelted us
with answers. Whatever tears we had were pressed
like olives. He came quietly then,
a stirring in the frost, a shuffling of the lamb's feet.
When the cold settled on His eyelids
it was as if a flock of doves lowered their quilt
down around us. It was then we knew that
the stars only wanted to drink from the pools
they seemed to live in, or become the insects
you could hear above the heartbeats of animals.
It was like lifting a stone to see another world,
a stone we had carried all that time.
Now the whole story will appear like the exposed roots
of a dogwood. Hope collects like dew in the desert night.
Even the hanged man will strangle his ropes.
It is our swords that will plow the sky.
Our lives are thumbprints in the air, which means
that soon all our dreams will wander on without us.
Our graves will fill their sails with light.
You can open their words like almonds.
You have to step into that river that flows inside you.
It is a world where suns are sown like seeds.
It is not easy, this beating your wings against the world.
Even now you can see the fingertips of His words
starting to knead the air into the shape of a prayer,
a sentence inscribed in your eyes that only you can read.

Nicodemus' Dream

Night was still dripping from the leaf tips.
I thought at first his words just littered
the ground. I had wanted to know
why we should believe anything
beyond the realm of the stars. All my dreams
belonged to someone else. What he gave me was
a way of dreaming from the insides of trees,
from the bottoms of clouds. It was like the lonely call
of the doves, the way the morning moon becomes
one with the sky. His words were metaphors
for other words, so that my dreams became
metaphors for other dreams. Every Religion is
a dream we try to believe. No way is really
the way. But I can tell you it is not any god's way
when you blow pieces of each other into bizarre
constellations. It is not anyone's word when
believers dream their own dreams as truths.
Each of those dreams only gives birth to another dream,
another beheading, or rape or gas attack.
If only we could hear the timeless echoes
that reach us from beyond the farthest ends
of the universe. Even your scientists know
they ride on gravity waves from the birth of everything.
It is a language of love giving birth to other loves.
Now I understand how each drop of rain must be
destined for its spot on the earth, how each shard of
sunlight must have a shadow to brighten. I am still
not sure what it is I heard Him say. You have to
doubt what you believe and believe what you doubt.
You have to work each long furrow of the heart whose
seeds will surprise you like the hidden stars of daylight.

Dorca's Second Life

Matthew 9:25; Mark 5:40, 41

Everyone wants to ask their questions of the dead,
but I can't tell you what it was like for me—
I saw no lights to guide me, no heavenly sounds.
Just a voice saying "Get Up," and I got up.
Then I was alive again with something to believe.
That was when the ocean revealed shades of
color I had not noticed, when the olive tree
seemed to welcome me as part of whatever
it belonged to, when I could almost hold the air
in my hands. It was as if I had the many eyes of a bee.
It was as if the story of my life had changed.
Everyone has a story, most of it what they hope
will show them best. It's a question of Truth.
I can hardly explain what I am or was. My Greek
name means gazelle, a sign we took for beauty,
but I wasn't special. My Hebrew name was *Tabitha,*
the name of a princess in Judah, but I was
no princess. It was enough to do what I could in Joppa.
I don't understand this need I see to boast, to rally
some fickle crowd with what they want to hear. Everything
passes so quickly. In many ways your life is like
those brief Mayflies if you compare them to eternity.
That's why I can't understand all these lies,
this "trash talk" as you call it, even from your leader.
I could tell you it all comes around, but it doesn't.
Some men simply are not men. Some are swine.
I could tell you there is nothing to gain, but there is.
For now. When we first climbed out of the trees
everything changed, but some remained there
thinking they were above the law. Some, as I see it,
are still there. Remember the Truth is inside you.

Remember your life is a one-time gift, not
the second chance I was given. Remember
your life is like that shimmer on the distant
desert floor you can't quite decipher, but must try.

Zaccheus' Testament

Word spread like the branches of the sycamore before He ever
arrived. The wind was hoarse with meanings more urgent than
I had never heard. It was as if we were living in a time no one
had ever measured. The branches pointed randomly like the hands
of a broken clock. Every word was a question whose answer
hovered like a dragonfly. My herd stopped and turned in unison
as if it understood. Whatever I was roosted in the tree beside me.
It is hard to name exactly what the change was. I thought I had
somehow been born in another language. What I had saved
meant nothing. It was as if my life had been lived somewhere else.
Yes, there were these streets, the books I kept so carefully,
the clients, the markets, the temple, the rising sun, the falling sun.
My own story was never worth mentioning except as a symbol.
This is all I can offer for I have been watching the couple
by the side of the road holding a sign whose words seem as broken
as they are, I have seen the refugees washed up on your shores
like driftwood, the tent cities, how one war stands in line behind
another, one river poisons another river. I want these words
to spread like an echo. I want the old truths to emerge from
the caves of the souls that have hidden them, to spread like
the branches of my sycamore. We had to learn to ignore
what the Prefect told us. We were all foreigners to him.
Every dream we had flowed into the next until there was a sea.
It is the same way now. For you. If only you would believe.
Whatever has not yet happened has already happened.

Thomas' Blindness

That was years ago, a time when flocks of gulls
seemed to flap through my head. Everything was
its own promise. But what was really there?
The future seemed to explode
like one of your mortar shells. The vines flowered
briefly but no squash appeared. All that Spring,
the insects were questioning my face.
I could hear the bones of brush clatter in the wind.
With these fingers I pulled back the folds of His wound
like a billfold. I should have believed. It is hard
to believe our words that tell us only what took place
in the past. Now as I walk through the words for field,
for mountain, let the word for moonlight shift
among the orange trees, the word for shadow lean
like a hobo against the rocks, how could I know
what they meant to do? How they meant not
field but emptiness, not mountain but distance,
not moonlight or shadow but hope and despair.
It is our own guilt the dogs sniff out along the roadside.
Who led me to these cliffs or where I should go,
I can't say, but I can dream the town below,
the streets orderly as fishnet, the women
whose fat hangs from their arms loose
as the bellies of clams. I know, but can't see
how moonlight chalks the water.
How either silt pours from the river or
the eels are running again,
how shells of boats barnacle the beach, wishbones
the seas in winter broke. Even now, there are
these little blisters of sound that reach my ears.

For instance, the gulls that pester returning boats
like moths around a light. And there is
that sound of shovels
scraping against bone as they dig up
the graves of the victims no one believed from Kosovo.
Old enough to confuse dream and eyesight, I'm afraid
that my own dream might also fail
or that it include someone known
washing in the surf like seaweed. Will that be me
dreaming my life? I can feel the backhand of the light
brush over my face or maybe it is a dream
like His voice that burrows, still, into the cliffside.
Our sins start with something as invisible as lice.
The years are forgotten notes that slip from our pockets.
It is time to read those notes. It is time
to listen for the echoes of what you once believed,
a time still shivering in the trenches.
The time He took, the time He made more real.

The Apology of Judas

In those days I could fold the sky up and store it
in a closet. With every heave of my chest
the universe seemed to expand. In those days
the rope of the moon floating on the surface
of the water was a kind of hope. I hardly noticed
the bird's song limping from its broken nest,
hardly noticed the last star struggling against
the dawn until the sun betrayed it. Why do
we notice so little? Does the river suffer when
you plunge your hand into it? Does the wind suffer
when it snags itself on a branch? Maybe that's why
we close our eyes to kiss. I think each night was just
the bandage I used to cover the deep cuts of His words.
Don't turn away. Don't imagine you know the story.
Our lives are just dreams someone sold to the
highest bidder. I thought my own words could
trample the stars. I thought my name would nest
in the future and take flight. But there was only
that dusk of blackbirds. It's all just Fate settling
like dust in the attics of our deeds. But why
were they surprised? Why was a sword drawn?
Why has a sword always been drawn? Why do we
turn away from all those bodies of children bulldozed
into Bosnia, or the nursing mothers whose breasts are
cut off with machetes in Liberia just to deny the future?
Maybe we have to betray ourselves in order
just to be ourselves. In the end, Truth taps
at the windows of our souls. What quivers on the lake
are only the footprints of Fate. Even our astronomers
hear the funeral sounds of dying galaxies before they
ever see them. Gusts of time are filling my lungs.

They all said I was just a small part of the plan,
that they hold no grudges, no plans for revenge.
Then why is there such a haze over my heart?
I'm the crow the hawks chase from their nests.
I used to think Love would protect us from the shadows
we cast. I used to think that Hope was not what
jingled in our pockets. I used to think all this loneliness
would be unbearable. Now each word is a betrayal,
is the frayed rope-end of desire. Everything I say is
like some cargo hidden in the hold of a sunken ship.
In the end we all learn there's no sea, no sky, no word
big enough to hold all our pain. Only this kiss. Only
love's dragline already hooking the very thing it fears.

The Centurion's Plea

Matthew 8:5-13

Through flocks of rain a single wing of light flickers
an intermittent yes and no. Or that forgotten lighthouse
beacon sends a feeble warning that seems to arrive
out of the past. Some invisible clanging buoy redefines
what we mean by distance and time. It wants to lean
with the tide that is about the change. We put on
the night like a sailor's slicker. The jagged shoreline
keeps tempting the sea. Everything is a temptation.
I called on Him when my servant fell paralyzed,
and He came despite what the neighbors said.
It was His way. Everyone was deemed worthy.
True, I commanded many, but he commanded the wind.
Back then I did not understand the *outer darkness*
But now, in your world, I see a quivering thread of
this new morning's stained air is about to uncover
smudged bruises of light and shadow. I see the driftwood
from a boat that is clambering to climb the rocks. Soon
the gulls will come and go like a sudden realization
rising inside us. This is the moment that keeps returning.
The watchman turns towards the sound that was always there.
The clouds change disguises but remain the clouds.
The rocks are weathered but remains the rocks.
The waves lie down into their own stories. Mistaken
at a distance for plastic bottles, a few bodies slosh
against the rocks. The wind hushes their secrets.
Did you think what I said had nothing to do with
the refugees who were drowned? We are all outcasts.
We are all part of someone else's plan. All we have is
what we are, what we try to be. It is not important where
our truths arrive from, only that they are here, like
limbs pointing in every direction asking for nothing.

Now the fog comes in to cover what the rains could not.
It is not too late. There are more miracles than you know.
Tomorrow retreats on the tide. The eye of the storm
always seems close before you can act on what you see.

Paul's Lesson

They say every belief is a prison but I have known
prisons. They say the soul is a punctured balloon.
At the sound of a trumpet they arm themselves
with hate. Their troops write histories of grief.
Their own souls became coffins. Who would begin
again in a world like that? I travel still in chains.
So much I wrote has been misunderstood. The real
leaders in Corinth and elsewhere were the women.
It was they who first arrived at the tomb. Everyone
focuses on a line or passage, but not the whole spirit,
not what it meant to the oppressed and the outsiders.
Every word is a question, every question a doorway.
My journeys have never ended. *Get in good trouble*
one of you said. That's why your faith still knocks
on the door. Forget those messengers who have forgotten
the meaning of their words. I remember the storms at sea,
the fear that drove men towards the unspeakable.
Sometimes the rain fell in needles. Sometimes the air was
charged with revenge. Yes, it was difficult to believe
through those nights dressed in despair. I was ready to
pronounce my own sentence. I was ready to hold
a sword or light the flame myself. You know. Not like
those who incite riots when you were only preaching
for peace, for the soul's freedom. I know. They always
seemed to come from a town we left. It is a hard thing,
what I ask in return. You can kill what you hate until
there is no one left in the vacuum around you. You can
poison the air with your own bombs. But you can also
turn away from those shadows of oblivion. The only real
borders are the ones we create in our hearts. You might want

to curse the moon. You might want to behead those who would
behead you. When you lift the sword above your head
remember what you have raised above you, how every
killing is a form of suicide. And how every love is a seed
but that what it brings is nothing you asked for, nothing
you didn't already have waiting behind the doors of your heart.

Luke: Just Listen

Everything that lives is Holy.
        —Blake

In some towns even the stones seemed to lie.
But under each stone a door to another world.
In some towns the shouts flew around the forum
like locusts. In other towns, whispers you could
hardly tell from the wind. The world is not
the world you think it is, its meanings tangled
in vines of fear. Just think of your colorful
Angel Wing Begonia whose petals are poisonous.
Just listen to the poisonous words that divide
you from the truth Paul prayed and preached.
It is as if the geese broke formation forever, or
as if the clouds continuously split from each other.
I don't have to tell you your own world has split
open like a false geode. The words of your leaders
are the empty shells of lizards. Their microphones
pollinate the earth with lies. But listen to this—
do not fall into divisiveness. We are all hybrids.
All we knew then was to love each other as if
we were all one. We are all mongrels.
Just listen. The world is a parable if you listen
closely. Squirrels drop their nuts from the pecan
tree like secret messages from another world.
Just listen. There is a fungus, mycelium, that threads
like neurons connecting the trees so they can talk
to one another. This is the way one soul talks
to another soul. Listen. You that have ears, listen.
One night the cell doors opened. You know the rest.
There was a voice but no words, but we listened—

the cicadas' song draped across the branches,
even the ticking of the roaches, the scurrying
of the blind moles beneath us, the owl floating
overhead, even the lowly spider whose web
stiches the air around you are prayers meant only
for you, for now, and for the world you will become.

Junia's Name

Rom:16:7

It begins with a mustard seed and then you have
a twenty foot tree spreading out like a pinwheel
galaxy. With me it was centuries before they translated
my name as a woman. *I is another,* Rimbaud once wrote.
In place of me they needed a man because Paul
called me his fellow apostle and prisoner. It's like
someone dialing your number but insisting
your name is wrong. The tears are centuries old.
They look at the stars and invent their own constellations.
They don't see we are slowly devouring the dwarf galaxy
in Sagittarius while some other galaxy hunts us.
All that will be left will resemble a burnt-out haystack.
The low music of the cosmos will grow fainter.
But for now we are like the lost notes on an abandoned
guitar. Sometimes they like to think of us like those
no-see-ums that plague you. How many times
have our ideas wilted on their vines before they blossom?
Their words float by like tumbleweed, their histories
read like unmarked dirt roads. I am not sure how
to explain all this. There are worlds inside us
they will never know, like the Light that bends
so much we never know where it came from.
It hardly knows what to do with their world. Its stars
meditate on the origin of darkness. It is a history
you will have to write. But for now we are
like pages torn from a book. The search for
our history is the search for the soul. Be patient.
It took ages to rise from the sea. The sun leaves
both shadows and Light. You have to wait by moving.

You have to let the wind erase your footprints.
There are roads not visible on your maps. Pascal
thought the world was a funhouse where we become
an insect in one mirror, a giant in another. We are never
where we are. How often are we only metaphors
for what we want to be. I can tell you that what we take
to be stars are galaxies, and what we take as galaxies
are the thumbprints of God. But that is not what you want
me to say, to condemn their name for me. Just wait.
Time stammers by but says little we understand.
Everything is bigger than it is. All their words have never
changed the weather, nor will it change us.
They hold up babies and give speeches to faded
gravestones. They control the pronouns in a language
whose meaning holds little for us. They are the dark
spaces between constellations. Their souls wait for
the history like a deaf host waiting for his guests
to write down the meaning of their silences. See:
their words are beginning to fill each moment with
their own emptiness, their dreams wander through
darkened streets. The stars they thought the lake held
for them each night are already washing up on the shore.

Chloe's Oracle (Corinthians)

There is neither Jew nor Greek, there is neither slave
nor free, there is no male and female, for you are all
one in Christ Jesus.
                                            —Gal 3:28 (CEB)

That means you must also love immigrants
because you were immigrants in Egypt.
                                 —Deut 10:19 (CEB)

Sometimes your words are like litter picked up
off the sidewalk and pocketed until you finally
forget them, or like bits of paper ascending
in flame and turning to ash, or fog imitating
a dense smoke in a dead tree here, or like crystals
you grew in chemistry lab turning into something
unexpected, so too your words—disappear, only
to suddenly reappear in the midst of a dream
that occurs in the middle of another dream,
except that what it means soon lengthens its shadow
from the future back into past so that you don't know
where it, or anything, including you, began. If you
go back far enough there is a single molecule
that dreamt each of you, but you can never go back,
as even your James Agee said,—you must look ahead.

Today it's the future your Dreamers want that seems
to fly into the tree. It is like watching a flock of blackbirds
follow the leader in loops through the sky. Or the invisible
dark matter that is six times as plentiful as light
which means you live in a mostly invisible world.
So there's no reason one thing follows another,
wrote Hume, no way to know when or why you are.
With so many words for perches, the birds don't even
know where to land. It only matters that they sing.

74

Too often I have watched your future wash up
with the seaweed. Too many lives are like hermit crabs
that never find a home. Your skies are in a stupor.
There are so many sounds that eat their way through
your hearts. So many languages that fed your own.
All is one and that one is Divine, wrote Spinoza.
The static sounds from deep space, heard by accident,
were first rejected as foreign interference then embraced
as sounds from the big bang still hanging around on
the galaxy's street corners. But none of your mercurial
solutions seem to stay around too long. The dead tree
I see has probably been eaten from its insides
by Black Ants. When the limbs get ready to fall
they are called *widow makers.* At some point
you have to speak for everyone's dreams or they will
become so much mulch. We are all one, Paul wrote.
That means you have to turn those words into sanctuaries.
If not,—the future in a knot, a menagerie of conflicting
desires, the untied shoelaces of your histories.
Every sound of a branch falling is a knock at the door.
They listen to the unimaginable sounds their dreams offer,
the way a whole planet breathes through each object
or hushed word, the way a whisper echoes in a cave,
the brushing of oat against the wind, those words that mean
more than what they mean, scattering, just the way
our sounds will scatter with solar dust into unborn galaxies
where someone will hear, once again, their dreams
becoming a sentence, as story, a hope for love and peace.

Pricilla's Journey

Acts: 18

No one, at first, believes. No one thinks
it's worth dying for. After we arrived in
Corinth Paul appeared as if with the tide.
Words flew around us in flocks. It was
as if he could hold the wind on a leash.
We felt a spirit cover us like our tents.
We followed him until Ephesus, a city
where the sky seemed to hang as low
as laundry. If you want to believe
you have to follow the scraps of stars,
the way the hawk slices a path through
the evening light, the impossible routes
the planets seem to take, Nothing is
obvious, nothing is assured. At any
moment the hawk will fold its wings
and fall like an arrow into the neck
of whatever waits below. No one is
ever ready. There are signs if you wish
to read them, cross hatched in the sand,
or scribbled in the far mesh of stars,
but they are things you already know
in your heart, things you have to let free,
falcons that will begin their own search
for the truth that approaches without a sign.

Lydia of Philippi

—Acts 16:13-40

As with the slats in the blinds that let light in, or the holes
in your abandoned factories that release the souls of
all who worked there, we have to see through the gaps
in our thinking. I heard him as I went out through
the city gates towards the river for water. You knew
right away he was nothing like that false prophet
who worked for the tyrants who ran the town.
His words brought a whole landscape of mystery.
How easily he untied the knots of our despair.
Our own tongues had become roadmaps of hurt.
When they put him in prison the whole earth shook
and his captors put on the cloaks of hope. You have
your own tyrants whose lies cast spells that sound
like truths, whose gaps are not what let light in
but are the black holes that pretend to embrace you.
Trumpets of hate only need someone to play them.
We each have our own prisons. It's true, our brittle
lives can break apart on moonlight, and with each lie
whole galaxies collapse into grains of light. But
remember how each love sows its own universe.
Do not be like the hummingbird who hesitates.
Remember the nightshade has its own time for flowering.
Remember the crows chasing the hawks from their nests.
Every act of love is a life buoy for the soul.
Every kiss leaves a trail of broken chains.

Mary's Parable

Every morning the sun paused over the hills
as if it too knew what I wasn't ready to see.
Even then, each memory was a path crossing another
path like a fish net that captures only the passing currents.
Those mornings the shadows birds passed over me
carrying away so many moments that will never return.

What would you have done if you knew the end?
Who could really understand what it all meant?
What mother would not try to delay the passing
of seasons, not try to pluck the thorns from the rose?

But His words still hang in the air like the valley fog.
It is true, they hold so much that is unspoken. Like
the way it's impossible to describe the light as it
flexes across the desert's surface, or the way night
shadows seem more real than what they seem to image.

So too, it was only later that His words bloomed,
only later that I understood each story he told hid
a story that we are still trying to learn. What hurts
more than that story is what it has become for you.
It is not for you to pick the single bits and pieces
of what He said that suit the way you want to live.
You have to cast about your past. You were not
made in the image you have become. Each one
of you should be Him, but for you the homeless
are invisible, the poor cast aside like the lepers
of my own day. Your hungry live from dumpster
to dumpster. You slap your enemies with lies
and bombs. Surely, there is no one you love
more than yourselves.

I could go on, but let me
tell you a story: one morning I made my way
through the olive groves, the ground fog rising
nearly to the tops of the trees. I could hear, not see
the birds awaken, could almost hear the heat rising
from the dirt, could taste the rain that was about
to arrive, feel the light stroking my hands as
the fog lifted. I think the whole world held me
in its invisible, impossible arms, as if to say
we are all one, a mystery each sun tries to reveal.

Kelsay Books